Creature Comforts

Grace Cavalieri

Typography by Kathryn E. King
Book design by Ed Lyle

ISBN 0-915380-16-1
LC 82-51068

About the cover: The title of Mary Ellen Long's serigraph is "Suffering into Creation," from a poem by Grace Cavalieri, 1974. Mary Ellen Long has studied lithography and painting, receiving her MA in printmaking. At the present time, she is using photography, collages, and handmade papers to express ideas connecting the natural world, oriental symbols and her own ritual making forms. Her award-winning work is exhibited in galleries throughout the United States.

THE WORD WORKS, INC.
PO Box 42164
Washington, DC 20015

" . . . stay out of jail, get what I write
printed, eat regular, and get a little love . . . "

Carl Sandburg

Grateful acknowledgment to *The Washingtonian Magazine, Poet Lore, Kauri II, The George Washington University Review, The Washington Dossier, Baltimore Renaissance: Poetry, The Ear's Chamber.*

CONTENTS

The Child   7
Pets   8
The Social Elite   10
Creature Comforts   12
A Life of the Mind   13
Details   14
The Passersby   16
This Is   17
New York City   18
The Lansburgh Building   20
The Late Sun Burns   21
Feeling States   22
Transparencies   23
How to Obtain   24
Contexts   26
The Sufi Message   27
It Starts with a Feeling   28
An Illustrated Poem   29
Negotiations   30
In Every Sadness   31
Banging at Your Doors   32
Common Purpose   33
Lilah   38
Les Jardins   48
Points in Space   52
Lyrics for Kate   53

THE CHILD

Through the door there comes the child.
No, the doctor says, you may feel
Like a child but the reality is
You are not.
Send the child back where she came from,
Have you heard that if you give
Her something, she will give you more
In return? I remember this. I cut the
Thin white slice in half. There is
No lack of opportunity to do good
If you are willing to get nothing for it.
Give the child her half. Send her back.
Like the cats, she will slip behind the
Mirror able to get through a space if
Her ears can get through.
The gold surrounding the mirror assures its edge,
Framing it. The gold is
A saxophone, singing, crying,
Hear it crying against the snow outside
The window. The child is nowhere to be seen.

PETS

Remember when the cat
   was taken to the pound and
When we returned from our vacation
   there he was again
   on the stone walk
Waiting
   from having traveled miles
   across village and city
You think, then, that I can make
   the comparison?
The return, all soft and bleeding
   of all things lost?
Belief in
   the yellow cat
The bottles of perfume and polish
   lined-up on the dresser
   marriage, lovers
   fathers, mothers,
I ask the cat to
   please not fantasize in my presence
So afraid that what I love
   and what *it* loves
   are not the same.
It runs behind the hedge
   sits in the same place where it was
Clipped by the hedgecutter
   years ago,
   one sore still on his cheek,
Why did my cat sit still for it
   like that?
I can understand a disease for people
   like us
   in those days
To have a face eaten away but
   to wear it like paint? Well I got mad.

The doctor, though skilled, was
    just a man, with a terrible
    resignation to pain
I settled in, knowing to comply
    was best.
They'd have no trouble from me and the
    cut cat.
No hope, the doctor said. Nothing is possible
    and nothing works whatsoever. I asked
If he'd sell me the names of all
    the pets who loved their mothers.
He replied simply that he was not
    capable of analysis. All he asked
When I brought my animals
    was how much they cost.
If there is nothing you want from
    such conversation, it is very hard
    to continue.
Give my best to the curator
    he called as I ran clutching
    my poor animal.
Love yourself in your act! He called.
    Pain and imprisonment are magically
    returned
With the thought of the
    cat who traveled so far to get back to me.

THE SOCIAL ELITE

This pale grey and rose dress is my mother's
   returning to be dusted and hung
To be brought on stage and worn
   in the light
   like a singer.
Servants move silently among us,
   taking care of us without concern.
The maintenance man takes my dress
   to the cleaners and stops by the five-and-ten
To see if there is anything which
   can meet my needs,
He walks ten miles an hour. Without
   a car, you'll do anything to get a ride
   if you are intent on maintenance.
Since my father died
   I have no one to think about
   but the hired help.

The servants have no concern, yet
   they take care of us. They
Carry my thoughts on a platter. So unable to
   make a human contact, I say
"I'll buy my meals outside, thank you"
   the maintenance man fills my glass
   then drinks it
The meaner he gets
   the nicer I am.
We sit around a long dark table. The cut
   glass pickle dish is framed by death
Sitting in the center of the table
   as if we won't notice it.
   It is exactly out of reach.
No one asks to be served
   no one eats from it. It is put away.

Since my father died
   my hands move horizontal.
For the social elite, some emotions
   no one can help you feel. I cheered up
The dinner party saying DID YOU KNOW THE
   DIFFERENCE BETWEEN CASUALLY AND CAUSALLY,
The voice is such a tiny instrument
   no one else can hear and
   no one answers.

CREATURE COMFORTS

Although the older eye loses light
   the less it asks, the more
   we want to give,
Compulsive sight seeks connections
   such as flight and
   what else is there but
The bullfight, the accolades
   the crowds, the wine-
   skins,
      the flowers.

A LIFE OF THE MIND

I wanted to be held up to the window
To look out before
Everyone was leaving

When I told you that others
Mistreated me
You told me how to improve myself

Even so,
The irregular snow is an amazing
Combination of notes, separate like a guitar's

The cat and I are watching
I say THANK YOU to no one in particular
I say to the cat THAT IS SNOW.

DETAILS

Details are important,
How much salt you put on your food
Whether you eat half a grapefruit for breakfast
Details are the way we distinguish ourselves,

Say someone pulls out your back teeth
Then offers you steak
How much steak you are given is a detail
And milk in such small amounts
Not enough to make you sick, not enough
To make you well.

The taste of a man if his lips are bitter
The initials on his belt
These are the particulars. Especially
The way we wish to see the people
We've injured be happy,

And the way we correct ourselves
When we cannot correct others,
The crossing of the street, the speed
And the precision in being
The first in line at the red light
Or last in line at green,

The little things, like having an extra
Child. We thought for a time it was
All we deserved. To cultivate the details,
Wherever you are, go somewhere else,
Otherwise, the media will not discover you
Even if you send a full length picture of yourself to the editor,

There are little facts you must face
Whether you are a boy, whether
You are a man, riding
A bicycle or smoking a pipe
See the difference — Do it for your sake.

I found the tiniest thing about myself,
That way I could say I thought he didn't
Want me because it was Monday
Now I know he doesn't like me because it is Tuesday,

Try to be exact
Then eat something sour for grief
It is all connected.

THE PASSERSBY

It is already ten after eight and
Now they circle with their arms around me
Never touching. Someone offers to be my chauffeur,
Driving backward at ninety miles an hour
On a high highway in France.
I prefer coastlines. At home there,
I am grateful for the way the cat
Jumps on the table.
I close each closet door, making sure
The shades are even
Throughout the house. I begin to be alone.

My style will be starting each day
In a different way
As we do our paragraphs
Picking up rocks once impervious to love
Counting them like a dead man's money.

THIS IS

The September of our Loss

The old man who is to die
Takes a nap anyway

I admire that

NEW YORK CITY

I was reading a letter searching for love
They said What Are You
Looking For On The Page, I said:
Radioactive water, white
And thick where there is
A floating pillow
Carrying with us what we
Are worth
And in whose eyes,
She smiled a smile so sweet
I knew she'd never worked a day in her life
So happy she ordered
Melancholy for lunch thinking
It was a vegetable
All melted over with butter.
That night I went out for dinner
And had a small pot of expresso
With lemon rind floating and
A splash of anisette.
You fingered the glass without
Knowing it, the rim like a clitoris
Over and over
Turning everything into
A vulva casual like
Your elbow on the rail, easy
As a man who never got a rash,
I knew by the shining of your eyes
I'd never get rid of you.
I left control over my life
In a black plastic pillbox
At The Academy of American Poets
Or else I lost control there,
It was in a small case big enough
To fit in a purse with two compartments.
You said I was European
You said I had a safety device
You said you were jealous.

I strained the pot of the last
Taste of my grandmother's kitchen,
In those days I thought everything everybody
Said was the truth,
I kissed her dog and left.

THE LANSBURGH BUILDING

Never mind that he gave
His new love
Twenty thousand dollars
Your father left you.
The dancers are here
In reds and purples,
The piano player is kind.
I say "Do you realize that
Going up the stairs sounds exactly
Like going down,"
I go down and I do not return.
The dancers say the less surface
Your feet touch the better,
That if you move your knees forward
A lot of other things will happen.

THE LATE SUN BURNS

(five poems)

If you are going to fall
With glass in your hand
Drop the glass

*

There's nothing left to share

*

Your smell still on me

*

A night flood of goodbyes or
Is it this flower on my sheet

*

You can feel what you feel
There's no one waiting

*

FEELING STATES

The penis is an appendage
Which listens.
No mind of its own
It moves when beckoned,
The spirit goes as far out
As it goes in.
Do not blame the penis
For the man.

TRANSPARENCIES

This is about itself
It is not about anything else
It is not a statement about
A dead lady in a gold
Powdered face
Overcoming reason
With love fading cold.
If I talk of birthdays
I mean fluttering and whispering
And candles burning melancholy.
That is enough to say.
Feathers, faint and sprawling
Like fleece sink to
The sea.
The slant view *is*
A view.
See that willow tree ruling
Like a giant?
That is about itself
And therefore is about
Drifting stones in paper
Gardens and everything
In between,
How total is a star?
How afraid?
If I say its edges, once perfect
Fall like heat in our eyes
Plunging loss
Isn't that enough?

Angels shine in hell like nails
Across yellow tides. They
Privilege us with that first
Death we saw.
Glittering
That too is about itself.

HOW TO OBTAIN

It'll happen when you least expect it
Turning on its socket toward you
On its edge through air to meet you
Gleaming, when you least think it will happen
When you are lifting your leg like a
Stripper, the stocking shining and bright
Something will come your way—right then
When the priest
Puts a small sun on your tongue
When it is high holiday
When the chicken is cut in half
And a green wilderness pops out
You will notice it
You will start seeing it
One day it'll finally
Come to you, payment in full
The way we mark our calendars
With different days or
The way we want to share a sound
The publicity subcommittee will reach out
To you before you know it
One morning when it seems they won't look at your cooking
And then at night they can't praise your food enough,
It'll come to you the way the songs we sing ourselves,
Humming under our breath, always tell the truth
When the moon goes down
When you're playing crazy eights
When you're telling a friend what you think
Or at the moment right before you call out the police
Or before your worst fear attacks you, working
Its buttocks like a brown horse
Before the spoon sinks into the jelly dish
While the sun is still on your sleeve
As the dog moves from under the window

In a flash
In a kiss
In the distance between further and farther
The payoff will come to you saying
Something that cannot be learned
Quick as a twig
Crisp as a two dollar bill in the jewelry box
Shot through the heart with self knowledge
Before you can say Bobolink, Yellow Warbler
Violet green swallow, you will know it
You always knew it
The inside person and the outside person
Become the same
Like an immigrant traveling wrinkled and free
You will show them what you need
And tell them what you want
And of dying you will say
"Is this all there is to it"
You'll have known it all the time.

CONTEXTS

The cats want to be touched where
They cannot reach
Under the chin. They want
To go to sleep where there is
Nothing at stake.
What did you expect? They do not fear
Autonomy or buying their own stamps,
This is why you can see them dancing
Around the poles outside the hotel.
You do not see them changing partners,
They think in their own terms
They do not need to learn the steps.

THE SUFI MESSAGE

for ALICE

This is the poem promised us
On a street of yellow leaves
Where children run out,
It is better than the last poem
And therefore speaks of eternity,
It is an act of God
Like the insurance men said of my car
Which caught on fire. "Technically
No one's fault," they said.

When we go back to writing
We are always surprised
To be exactly where we left off and
Only as good as the last message heard,
Which in this case instructs us—
To find a quiet room
To breathe in through the crowns of our heads
And in breathing out
To focus on the heart.

IT STARTS WITH A FEELING AND THERE ARE WORDS

With respect to the horizon
Its illusion   I am walking my
        bicycle up the hill
Sometimes thought
Of a picnic basket with the plaid
                                spread
Inside and
Over the top, although one never existed
I prefer it from pictures alongside the
                girl with a floppy bow
As with all old
Thoughts   colors real and nothing like a
Remembrance of an old fantasy for recall
                delicious, distilled indirect
                bright
With respect
Think of the picnic basket
Light scattered by the dust making big birds
                seem the same as small
In this, approach is everything
Behind me
Apple trees budding like brides
                        way back in the forest
Essences   credulities   fugues
        remembering something
With the skill and the luck of a hunter.

AN ILLUSTRATED POEM

Just as if you are mentioned in a poem,
It will be forever more impossible
To know the relationship to the idea
Of the model on Martha's Vineyard perhaps
Or Southampton, how her husband
The lean lawyer must go up on weekends.
The model in The New York Times will
Never know the action line
To her reader
Even if she reads this poem and
Especially then she will not know I have
Fallen in love with her husband, his hair
Slightly curling, the way he tucks in his shirt.

NEGOTIATIONS

He buys a boat
I like the condo

I love to cook
He eats out

We take lessons
We both change partners

We go dancing
Each tries to lead

Downhill skiing or
Covering the court

He says "Let's move to Florida
Then we'll be happy"

I say "Let's be happy
Then move to Florida."

IN EVERY SADNESS THERE IS A FANTASY

The parallel view standing alongside the
Room he was inside
The way I was outside
The dialogue with the vest and the shoe
                                    by the bed.
                    This
Dream of rooms keeps me searching for
The island with the mountain of
Well being   Its houses so beautiful
A place where children
Can go near the water
                          When I sleep at night
This view of a dream keeps me
The way you keep me
Believing this by saying   Don't you have
Anything better to dream about?

BANGING AT YOUR DOORS

It is true the old dog limps on
Three legs where I proceed ringing
A bell,
In my eyes there's very little wrong
He can do
He howls
At the sky
Not caring even if it seems unattractive!
Shut
The shutters and
He bites:

       The lady I invited to dinner
       Who showed up in a ripped
       Nightgown and hairnet

       The petite burglar who tried on
       My clothes

       The old man who paid the girl
       A quarter to look

       The landlord who would not smile at me

You dare kick this dog?

Oh no. He trots at my side unsteadily
Ready to break out to a run
He knows my feet
By two pairs of shoes
One for Winter
One for Spring.
He is vulgar, unkempt
He farts
Against the wind
I'd trust him with my life.

COMMON PURPOSE

There are
Buzzards
By the church steeple
Two
Figures outside
A white church
This is serious
The birds collapse so
We will
Not believe
They could victimize others
They screech and die
I have
Been taught
A lesson
In every language

Thirty thousand centuries
Of animals
Are fitted to hunt
For
A sense of family
Creation
And
Destruction
Are our equal
The group
Our
Greatest weapon
Giraffes
Fight with their necks
Marauders like us
Make war on
Our own kind
Calling it
Common
Purpose

The pearl
Is on
The pillow
The ribbon
Ties
Our hands
Things like this happen
Among victors
Inconsistent delicacies
Like
Prayer
Are of no use to God
He was enthroned
To pay the price

Let us
Take off our faces
For now
Wear other masks
Up in
The valley
There are enemies
Killing each other
To keep
Our peace

Running
I run to you
Saying it hurts
If you
Are going to
Harm me
Moral supremacy
Is
An advancement
On our city
The fire
Is an illusion

If you are ruthless
How
Can I stop you
If
You are not
How can I make you
Be anything
Different
See how the dark
Picks up threads
Your body
Lifts off me
As if I were some great
Trouble
You
Could not
Bring yourself from
Feeling
Good

Love is the taste of water
Robots dancing
In a
Circle
When robots walk in a square
I
Close my eyes to you
Perhaps causing pain
This
Is
My holy weapon of peace

The
Dripping water
Makes
Some sonic sounds
One
By
One
Causing
Crass obedience calm
Now
After the war
What you wanted to do
One day
Was die
What
You did was
Win a war

You
Lower your voice
When you answer
I
Have to ask you
Twice
Can I go
Breaking
Statues
Climbing
Ropes
Escaping
I am shot
In the heart
Like a human
Or
Like
A medium size star
Broken
By space

The stick
With spikes
Bites
My
Left hand
I remain operational
While
You
Bandage my back

In
This ecclesiastical court
Someone
Is watching
We remain indifferent
To absolution
Our virtue
Is
The careful
Stacking of the coals

In the deciduous Autumn
Machines
Are no longer tools
They fade and die
There is a good chance
Of rain
In years to come
We'll laugh about it.

LILAH

for Bill

How to make the complex
From the simple
She thought
For the first time looking older
Than she was,
The sky also white and
Love not now immediate.

Perhaps if she could write
Everything she knew
On one piece of paper.
She looked at the bed where
The Black man lay.
Waywardness was a detail of
Life she expected,

"But I am Black too," Lilah
Thought
"There in the back of my heart."

Once he had said
"You know why you are happy
And I am not?
Because I treat you
Better than you treat me."

And of death thoughts . .
She had heard were simply worries
About money. That's all. So
She shouldn't leave about money
No, not about money
Maybe a plane ticket, but
Flying in fury across the
Country like that, no,
It would never do
Even our diseases aren't
Isolated anymore. No plane trips
No.

The sound of the water running
Next door
The sound of the scriptures
On a radio
Across the way,

The death of being poor
And
The butterfly here caught
In this case
That's where
The vanity of escape
Will get you.
A butterfly
Lives less
Than a hippo
But here it was under glass
All the same.

Snow fell on the ledge. Today
One could even
Be grateful for the frostbite.
The man moved. Lilah said
"I want somebody so bad, I don't
Know what to do. I want a real
Home with the smell of toast in
The house.

I want to be well groomed."

Then humming a song which came back
"Shall we proceed with the grief/
The weeping willow/
The loneliness of the neighborhood/
No need to hurry/
Let's put an end to guilt/
As for love/ My curiosity/ is satisfied."
The last part
She said
Out loud.

But there were reasons why she
Couldn't leave.
"We've suffered equally. I didn't
Take more than my share." He had
Told her the secret of love
"Even if it comes from outside
of yourself, let it love you." He
Called it LAYING ON THE GOLD.
Once she had dreamed
That he gave another
Woman all his love and a ten
Dollar bill besides.

Now she could go.
She wanted to be deeply
Connected to something like he was
But this was not her home.
Lilah didn't know where to
Keep the buttons and the thread.

Every night
She slept on one side of the
Large square bed—dreaming of
Going to London. Her man
Dreaming of his two-year-old son
The beautiful darkskinned mother
His deep rootedness causing her to
Cry out some nights—sitting straight up
Crying out,

"What is that, Baby," the man's
Voice said,
She started shaking (Be silent.
Remember The Nursery Rhyme:
"If you are good to the ghosts,
They'll be good to you") and then
He fell silent too.
Her goals were modest.
Her hopes for possible
Attainment could never work
In this one dark room.

She thought the man looked like
A tired old black bear with
Broken heart lines
His two eyes closed on his face
Like that,

Out in the park a child would
Be dancing in the snow with a
New balloon,
Lilah knew she could walk out
While he was sleeping
She wrote him a note, "I got a
Twenty dollar bill in my hand
Thinking of you."
There. That would do it. Did he
Think she was dumb? No. She
Was too old to be dumb.
Too dumb to be disappointed?
She knew what he owed her,

With the next man
She'd start over
Use dental floss
Be good —
Quit drinking and smoking
Write a letter to Ann Landers
Objectify the problem.

Sitting in a chair
She felt the old water rising. From
The water came chiffon,
Her mother's sleeves — Her
Father coming home to the
Kitchen
Her mother's hair up—in braids,
Her father drinking iced tea
In the kitchen
The big sleeves — soft and blowing
Flowers on chiffon — fading.
The man sat up in bed and
Called her name —

Lilah didn't answer
He fell back to sleep. Then
An old line "You know the
Love you didn't give me? Well, I'm
giving it to somebody else"

She corrected herself.
No. "You know the love you didn't give me?
I'm taking it back."
She stood up "Thanks
For the ride
I'm going farther on my own."
Or was it "further"
She never could remember.

The question being whether or not
One can change the existing structure.
He had freed her To express herself
But that was not enough at all —
Oh no not at all
Black men were connected
Deeply connected to an ecstasy
She didn't know or understand.
She was afraid to go because
If she walked out on him, this
Struggle, where was her raft
When she met the next river.
She knew if she stayed, she
Would thicken like other women
Do.

Living without resolution—without
Insistence, She'd finally had sex
With love
And It was better than without,
She thought.

She had come to him after
A rape on the street, almost
Two years ago next week—
She'd been raped by one man
And had a baby by another
Now gone—now dead and gone—
"I'd have left him flat then but . . . "

Emotionally barren Lilah had
Come to life in this one small room
Tiny and blonde
Like a glittering anomaly
On Chicago's South Side.

She knew it'd be all right, now to
say "move on"
There were chicken necks in the
Freezer and he could make himself
A soup,
"Where are you going" he said
Outloud
"Out."
"Out where."
"To give up everything I might need."
He said, "I don't mind if you
Leave me."
Lilah said "Thanks,"

"I just don't want you telling me
About it.
Now, where did you say you were going?"
"Nowhere," Lilah said. "Nowhere."
"You been walking loose again?" He said
"No, I've been here in the
Room the whole time."
"You been saying your Hail Mary's
Again?" Now he laughed
"Yes." Wasting my breath
"You coming back to bed now?"
"Yes," she said, buttoning up her blouse.

Life without him. Without
Shame and without passion . . .
But it's not me he's rejected—It's
My love
The worst thing a man could reject
She thought
She stood over him and looked down at
His dark face
"I want to hurt you because
You mean so much to me,"
She said simply.

He was quiet—then "Baby, there is
Nothing else to get."
Lilah whispered "Goodbye.
I didn't make your dinner and I
Didn't bring your dog the bones."

She looked down at her own small
White unthinkable feet—
Her loose robe
Her thin white arms
His wide face—with its deep tears
"Who are you" he said
"I am the woman with the
Dead baby at her breast
Who wouldn't give it up."
He reached out to her
Lilah felt as if the earth
Were being brought up to meet her,

Even if we had a perfect marriage
We couldn't tell each other
What we need.
His arms. His arms.
"What do you want?" he said
Soft
"Gimme all your money," Lilah answered.
He surrounded her like a magic box.

LES JARDINS

See the cold birds
By the red brick boathouse near the water
Their cold beauty
Disguised like a motive,
Small birds in the door in the wall,
Where the answer lay.

Someone is whistling. It is dark.
It is the man overpaying the bill
Then apologizing to the barmaid.
I mistook the light for sun and closed the door.

Who can say his gesture is from love?
And that it is to wrap his hands in silk
And to stroke his arms that he does such things?

Matters are not what they seem to be
Or as we wish they were.
Take the barmaid,
The blonde keeps sacrificing herself
Acting dumber and dumber and getting
Farther and farther from what she is feeling,

Lighter and lighter, her head is surrounded
By a halo of light, but now, fully mechanized
Her actions and feelings not one,
The voice gets higher and higher. Her anger lowers,
Cutting the girl in two.

Her head spins about from down the street. She
Complains that the rest of her body would
Wake her up to reject her. "I'm going to grow
And paint my fingernails," she calls back to herself.

She decides to be happy
She decides to be angry
She plans to move to the red brick boathouse
By the water
To feed the cold birds.

Her customer intends to cancel
His subscription to *The New Republic*
In order to express his needs and his rage.

They give each other a Christmas present
Then throw it out with the tissue paper,
If they had enough they wouldn't worry
About what was lost
She thinks her mind is trying to kill her body
He wants to pay her for a kiss,
"My feelings are my lips," she says.

Years later I passed a pile of old clothes
And knew they'd come that way.
The blanket
Holding all that was warm from them.

Placing a book on the ground, I hid
To see who would pick it up to read,
They came into sight
He said it was entitled: THE RICH OUTPOURINGS
OF A FERTILE MIND
She said it was entitled: THE RICH IMAGININGS
OF A GREAT MIND.

If I could only say what I felt for them
I'd say nothing.
The blonde barmaid said "I would hate anyone
To feel the way about me that I feel about
Everyone else."
Her customer jumped into the air and clicked
His heels.

Lately the barmaid and her customer stay
In a penthouse near the water.
The trick is to get to the window from
The top floor and crawl down
The outside wall from the roof and then
Invite everyone over for Thanksgiving dinner.

The nurse told her that, if in making love
The perspiration from his forehead went into
Her nose and up to her brain, the baby would be
Born intelligent. Afterwards she asked
The nurse why her body ached. The nurse said
"I don't know" and moved her off the bed
For the next patient.

Sometimes I will catch just a glimpse of
Them, the front of his sweater or a part of her skirt;
The way her skirt catches on her leg
And it will make me love them, but just for a brief
Second and just for that time,

Cheer up. Whatever they feel now, they'll feel
Something else later.
Do you want some orange juice?" He said and
She said "No thank you."
At the table he said "I didn't know she
Wanted some orange juice." I said "I
Didn't either." He said to her "I'm sorry,
I didn't hear you say you wanted some orange juice."

I thought I saw myself across the room
And excused myself but it was only
The barmaid wearing a white gown,
Her hood was empty. She sat on the chair,
Her hood fell off. She fell on the floor,

She is dead, I thought. I rushed
Back to tell them, to ask what
Part of myself she represented, such a
Versatile instrument, such a curious set of
Circumstances, not my feelings nor my defenses,

But something in between. The customer and the barmaid
Claimed that nothing I did happened,
As a guest, they put me to sleep in the mud,
My thumb pulled outside a hole in the board for air,
It grows crooked to this day.

One day I woke and said I smelled something awful on me
Like mud,
They said, No, We held you all night in our arms with
Love by the red brick boathouse near the water.

POINTS IN SPACE

for Robert

How shall we travel together? It is so long.
Proportions are high agreements, swimming freely full,
Passionately felt; these are the sources
Of our poetic conspiracies.
Experience measures the lyric balance,
Fence to gate, hinge to lock, with its
Embodied air.
For my people, our friends, the poets,
Spring was designed without bondage of visions.
There are dreams of children running toward us
Where nothing is dead,
Crowds are elsewhere.
Cities are laid out in feathers of rain
And good sun where
We are building our houses and
Telling the same stories, except for the words.

LYRICS FOR KATE

Don't depend on me for your
Soul. It
    may not be everything but with-
    out it you're nothing. Well
What'd you expect from
    someone who'd start a poem
    with "Don't."
Found in the attic with food
    in your hair, now in leather
Gloves
    halfway down the stair, using
your freedom like a cage,
Goddamnit
    Kate, you've forgotten everything I've
Ever told you.
Somewhere people are sitting in a
    sidewalk café
    maybe at 23rd and K, drinking
A glass of tea, unafraid to talk of
    escaped pleasures and
    self inflicted wounds without
This angry bargain of a friendship.
The minute we got mad at the blues singer
    I knew we were fed up with the pain
    and only one thing to do with
A habit
    break it and begin again. If
    the tooth is going bad, yank
It out. No sense worrying day and night
    about it.
The way your elbow touched his chest
I know how important it was to
    have a man's children
    (We always returned every favor.)
Like frogs who jump into a warm
Dark hole
    thinking it may be the pocket
    of a famous mountaineer
Who will carry us to the top,
    It may not.

Well what do you expect from a woman
    my age. This is how we talk. We
    have to because you won't
Listen. If
    you say "huh?" you can hear!
    and I'd gladly put it in the
Paper but who'd read it. There
    you go again, pre-
    tending I'm a man
When I'm paying the bill, you order
    everything on the menu and then
    say my plate looks good—
You won't leave me alone long enough
    to reject you. I beg for rest
    and you wake me up to say
You love me and that some people don't
    know what they need 'til they get it.
His skin was not friendly. He was not
    imbedded in the melancholy
    of time, like us who
Squeeze the grapes all day and
    get paid in wine at night but still
Remain curious enough to look at
The solar eclipse when told not to. Oh
    yes, life was simpler then
    complete with an 84 page
Handbook of hints and recipes,
Living through January with two kinds
    of men,
    the ones who loved the ladies and
The ones—
    you've guessed it again.
Trouble for us is crossing over this
Bridge without looking down
    trusting that metal reaches
    the other side,
Giving up worry that four children
    won't catch three fish
Until we're out of sight. "Kate,
    my name is Kate" is all

You'd say when I first met you. You
        were two people and I could
        only love one. Half of you
Copying the messages, the
        other half carrying the signs.
Would you rather wish on a star? Carry
        moonbeams home in a jar,
Or would you rather be Dan Rather
Wearing a suit that suits the occasion
        or do you want *HOPE* like two
Old ladies wearing braces
        and false eyelashes always
        walking with us. Well
To be tall is to be too tall
        but to be short and dumb
        these are two bad things. Let's
Not do it like the others, talking
        of nothing but auto accidents.
There's more,
        or all those poets
        wouldn't have made so much of it
        over the years
And the same goes for the people
        who started the Civil War.
Look. See there, the way the book-
        shelves fit between the windows,
        shows the world can be a
Friendly place. Anything you say will
        be appreciated not
        evaluated by detailed analysis;
We'll give some and take some and
        if we decide to go to The Lido
We can decide to go! Not figuring out
        whether they'll need us, whether
        they'll feel bad if we go, will
Be mad, will think badly of us. If
        we want to go (not confused
        by other people)
If we really want to go, we need
Simply, Kate, to go.

Grace Cavalieri is a poet and playwright. Her previous books of poetry are *WHY I CANNOT TAKE A LOVER*, *BODY FLUIDS* and *SWAN RESEARCH*. She is the producer/host of a longstanding radio program, "The Poet And The Poem," on WPFW-Washington. Currently she is media consultant to The National Endowment for the Humanities.